Original title:
Timberline Tales

Copyright © 2025 Creative Arts Management OÜ
All rights reserved.

Author: Tobias Sterling
ISBN HARDBACK: 978-1-80567-253-1
ISBN PAPERBACK: 978-1-80567-552-5

Glades of Remembrance

In the glades where squirrels play,
They run and tumble every day.
A nut that's tossed, oh what a sight,
A clash of fur, a comical fight.

Old owls hoot with a wise old grin,
While rabbits hop, let the fun begin.
Nature's jesters, so full of cheer,
In these woods, there's nothing to fear.

Nature's Echo Chamber

In the canyon, a voice calls back,
A echo laughs, on the same track.
"Who's there?" the trees all shout,
With a chorus, there's no doubt.

A bear sings off-key, what a sound,
While bunnies groove on the ground.
The rocks chuckle, the breeze takes flight,
Nature's stage, what a delightful sight.

The Whispering Woods

In the woods where chatter thrives,
Trees gossip as the critters dive.
"Did you see that fox?" they say with glee,
Running fast, like he's in a spree.

A dancing chipmunk, filled with zest,
Steals a snack, now isn't that the best?
The whole forest joins in delight,
In this playful, whimsical night.

Treetop Reveries

Up high where the branches sway,
The birds discuss their lively day.
"I saw a cat, what a chase!"
They chirp and giggle, at a fast pace.

Squirrels chatter with nuts in tow,
Dropping acorns, just for show.
While a raccoon snickers from a tree,
In this kingdom, laughter is free.

A Song for the Cedar

In the wood where the cedar stands,
Laughter hides in its leafy hands.
Squirrels dance, their tails in twirls,
Chasing nuts, like tiny pearls.

Birds chirp out a silly tune,
Bouncing high, like a warm balloon.
Raccoons giggle in the night,
Moonlight glimmers, pure delight.

The branches sway like they are high,
Tickling clouds that float on by.
Every whisper tells a joke,
As laughter wraps around the oak.

So raise a glass to woodland cheer,
Where every creature finds good cheer.
Cedar's songs, a playful spree,
Echo through the forest free.

The Heartbeat of Fir

The fir trees pulse with giggles bright,
Sharing secrets of pure delight.
Beneath their boughs, the shadows play,
Where squirrels prank in a cheeky way.

Each needle sharp with stories bold,
Of jumpy goats and deer on hold.
Frogs leap loud, a splashy show,
While owls chuckle, wise and slow.

Sunbeams dance on forest floors,
As chipmunks race through twisted doors.
The heartbeat thumps, a playful cheer,
Each thud a rhyme that all can hear.

Nature's party never ends,
With whispering leaves and funny bends.
In the realm where the fir trees sway,
Laughter rules the woodland play.

Legends Among the Larches

Among the larches, tales are spun,
Of mischief made and lots of fun.
A rabbit's race, a turtle's pace,
In every corner, a comical face.

They bring the past with jesting glee,
Breezy whispers, wild and free.
A fox's grin, a badger's song,
In this shady realm, we all belong.

Each trunk adorned with youthful dreams,
Beneath the sun, a stream of beams.
Chipmunks chatter with a wink,
While wise old trees just grin and think.

The legends grow with every tale,
As laughter dances on the trail.
In larchy woods, the spirits shout,
Share your joy; let laughter out.

Murmurs of the Moss

Soft moss carpets a giggling ground,
Its green whispers are all around.
Tiny critters throng the way,
Making mischief in bright array.

A snail slips by with a bashful smile,
Riding on leaves for a little while.
Frogs appear with jests galore,
Singing loudly, begging for more.

The mossy tales, a cozy nest,
Where laughter dwells and guests are blessed.
Grumpy mushrooms raise their heads,
As tiny beetles shout their threads.

In the hush, the chuckles grow,
Nature's jokes begin to flow.
In a world where the mossy laugh,
Every moment becomes a gaff.

Secrets Woven in Bramble

In the thicket, whispers play,
Bramble vines have much to say.
Squirrels gossip, owls debate,
While rabbits plan their dinner date.

A hedgehog's wearing quite the crown,
Dandelion fluff, a royal gown.
Bees drop by for evening tea,
Plotting how to steal the spree.

Underneath the leafy green,
Raccoons turn into quite a scene.
Magic hats and tails so grand,
They dance together, hand in hand.

So come and join the woodland jest,
Where secrets live and laughter's best.
In bramble's grasp, life's never tame,
Every shadow knows a name.

Footprints on the Forest Floor

Paw prints crisscross, a playful dance,
Bunny leaps with a stylish prance.
A fox with swagger, tail held high,
Winks at birds that flutter by.

Scratches in the dirt tell tales,
Of midnight meetings and funny trails.
A squirrel steals acorns with flair,
While deer try their best not to stare.

Mice gather crumbs for a feast so grand,
Spilling seeds like a careless band.
Every footprint is a clue,
To the mischief that animals do.

So tiptoe through this lively spree,
Watch the forest, wild and free.
Each print a laugh, a giggle, a cheer,
Stories woven, season to year.

The Watcher Beneath the Boughs

Beneath the boughs where shadows creep,
A wise old owl pretends to sleep.
Peeking out with curious eyes,
He's a judge of woodland lies.

Foxes sneaking, quite a pair,
Plotting pranks without a care.
He hoots at their plans, a hearty laugh,
As they trip over a fallen path.

Twigs snap, a raccoon scrambles wide,
A junky hat worn with pride.
Owl knows all, yet keeps it cool,
As critters dance around the pool.

So if you wander, don't you fret,
Under the trees, you'll find the set.
For every laugh shared where shadows lay,
The watcher brings stories to play.

Sylvan Dreams and Moonlit Streams

Moonlight spills on twisted streams,
Where frogs croak out their silly dreams.
Fireflies dance in jolly glee,
Making the night a twinkling spree.

A turtle hums a sleepy tune,
While crickets cheer, beneath the moon.
Bats swoop down in silly dives,
Joining in for nighttime jives.

A heron says, 'What a show!'
As branches sway to and fro.
Laughing fish jump, splash and play,
In this whimsical nighttime ballet.

So wander deep where laughter beams,
In sylvan realms of moonlit dreams.
Where every shadow shares a grin,
And nature's joy begins within.

In the Heart of the Hollow

In the hollow where squirrels abound,
A raccoon once danced, spun around.
With a top hat made of an old pizza box,
He juggled acorns and laughed at the flocks.

A fox joined in, his tail in a twirl,
Ambitious to impress the nearby girl.
But tripped on a root, oh what a sight!
The whole woods erupted in laughter that night.

The Dance of the Dappled Light

Sunbeams winked through branches high,
As fireflies chuckled, oh me, oh my!
With a jig and a giggle, they lit up the air,
Making shadows of bunnies dance without care.

A butterfly flapped with remarkable grace,
Landing on a mushroom, it held its place.
A beetle then rolled by, wearing a hat,
And shouted, "You missed me, oh, imagine that!"

Voices Among the Verdant Giants

In the grove of giants, whispers grew loud,
As trees shared tales, proud of their crowd.
One spoke of a squirrel who climbed up so high,
He got stuck on a limb, oh my, oh my!

A crane, from a distance, honked in delight,
"Get down, little buddy! It's quite the height!"
The squirrel waved back with a grin so wide,
As the leaves overhead chuckled, side to side.

A Symphony of Roots and Branches

Under the oak, the roots hold tight,
While branches swing low in the fading light.
A moose played the trumpet, what a bizarre show,
Meanwhile, a rabbit tap-danced below.

With a beat that would make even owls groove,
The forest came alive, in a joyful move.
The raccoons clapped paws in chaotic cheer,
As the chorus of critters filled the night air clear.

The Tangle of Time

In the woods where squirrels race,
Time stretches like a tightrope space.
A rabbit thinks he's won the day,
While leaves chuckle in a breezy replay.

Old logs tell tales and start to spin,
Of gnarled roots and where they've been.
The pine trees snicker, wisdom accrued,
While acorns giggle, feeling renewed.

Branches sway like dancers bold,
With secrets of the forest told.
A bear trips over a wayward shoe,
While a raccoon grins, 'I knew he'd do!'

With every twist and every turn,
The trees share laughs and lessons to learn.
In this woodland where mischief thrives,
Time's a jester, and joy's alive!

Old Souls in the Grove

In the grove where shadows play,
Ancient trees join in the fray.
With twisted faces, they chat and poke,
Making jokes with each funny oak.

A wise old pine, with needles unkempt,
Told a story, the crowd was preempt.
About a squirrel who fancied a feast,\nAnd ended up dancing with a crazy beast.

The mushrooms giggle, all nestled tight,
As the moon rises, casting its light.
'Why did the tree go to a party?' they say,
'Because it was fond of a good cabaret!'

Old souls sigh, sharing a grin,
In the warmth of laughter, they all fit in.
With cracks in bark and stories to weave,
In the grove of humor, they'll never leave.

Canopy Whisperings

Up in the canopy, whispers take flight,
With breezes carrying jokes through the night.
The birds are jesters, their songs full of cheer,
Making mischief that all woodland can hear.

A cheeky woodpecker, with a tap-tap sound,
Sings of a squirrel who's lost and found.
He ran in circles, chasing his tail,
While a wise old owl just laughed without fail.

The leaves rustle softly in giggly delight,
As shadows waltz under the soft moonlight.
A raccoon wearing glasses gets lost in the lore,
As he tries to read why the pine trees snore.

In this canopy, laughs grow like vines,
Where tales twist and turn as if drawn by designs.
Nature's comedians, up high in the trees,
Share all their laughter with the very low breeze.

A Journey to the Heartwood

A journey awaits with laughs galore,
To heartwood's core, we'll explore.
The fungi giggle at every step,
As trees partake in a merry prep.

A beaver arrives, bringing a hat,
Says, 'Is it fancy? What do you think of that?'
While critters gather, planning a show,
With costumes stitched from the wild, you know.

A chipmunk's joke on a badger's clothes,
Turns into chuckles and playful prose.
They dance to the rhythm of rustling leaves,
In this heartwood party, no one ever grieves.

With every branch that sways and claps,
The forest bursts with chortling wraps.
A journey claimed by laughter's delight,
Where the heartwood hides joy throughout the night!

Spirits of the Underbrush

There once were some critters so spry,
They danced with the acorns nearby.
A squirrel in a top hat, so grand,
Declared he'd start a nutty band.

The rabbits would hop with delight,
While the owls just stayed up all night.
The raccoons played drums made of leaves,
And sang songs you wouldn't believe!

A fox wearing boots found a tree,
And said, "This fine venue is key!"
With beats from the bugs, it was clear,
The underbrush parties are here!

So if you hear laughter at dusk,
Just know it's the woodland's own musk.
For underbrush spirits, you see,
Are the life of this wild jubilee!

Whispers of the Wind

The wind told a tale with a grin,
Of a turtle who fancied a spin.
He rolled down a hill, full of glee,
And bumped into a giggling tree.

The leaves rustled secrets that night,
Of a snail that could dance in the light.
He twirled 'round the rocks, not a care,
While birds in the branches would stare.

The breeze carried off all their jokes,
While teasing the dips of the oaks.
"You'll never keep up with our pace!"
Giggled the gusts, a wild chase!

So if near the woodlands you roam,
Listen for whispers of home.
For the wind's got a laugh to unfurl,
In the quirks of the natural world!

Shadows in the Canopy

In the thicket, shadows goofed around,
Playing hide and seek without sound.
A raccoon with a mask, quite absurd,
Lost in the giggles of chirping birds.

A wise old owl perched with a smile,
Chastised the squirrel for skipping a mile.
"You can't outrun the darkness, my friend,
But with friends, it's a game without end!"

The shadows laughed as the sun dipped low,
Filling the forest with a warm, soft glow.
They painted the ground with a twist of humor,
Giant feet of a very large rumor.

So if you see shadows at play,
Know they're laughing the daylight away.
For mischief lives in the cool, cool shade,
Under the canopy, joy never fades!

Echoes of the Ancient Pines

Among ancient pines where whispers thrive,
The logs have their secrets, alive!
A squirrel told tales of a spry deer,
Who pranced while the rabbits would cheer.

The trunks held the laughter from long ago,
Of raccoons who juggled in quite the show.
The echoes of laughter, so sweetly blend,
In a forest where joys never end.

Each creak of the boughs joins in the fun,
As shadows stretch out and warm in the sun.
A campfire's glow lights their wild spree,
With marshmallow dreams in a pine tree!

So gather beneath these tall, old friends,
Where fun and mischief always extends.
For the echoes of pines hold dear to the heart,
Stories and laughter that never depart!

The Sigh of the Sycamore

In the breeze, the sycamore grins,
Whispers secrets of silly sins.
Squirrels dance on branches tall,
While acorns play a game of ball.

Beneath its boughs, a cat does nap,
Dreaming of fish and a comfy lap.
The tree chuckles, leaves all a-quake,
At every rustle, the world's awake.

A robin drops its bright red snack,
And gives a shout, 'Hey, watch your back!'
The branches sway in laughter's tune,
Calling critters to join the spree soon.

With every zigzag, sway, and swing,
The sycamore teaches joy's true bling.
Under its shade, fun never ends,
Nature's keepers and silly friends.

Moonlit Maple Muses

Under the moon, the maples shine,
With leaves so bright, like stars align.
A party starts with a rustling breeze,
    As owls giggle up in the trees.

They tango with bugs till dawn, you see,
While shadows play hopscotch, wild and free.
The fireflies join with a flickering light,
Creating a show that lasts through the night.

A deer bursts in with polka dots galore,
While raccoons jive on the old forest floor.
A chorus of laughter, oh what a sight,
As tree trunks sway to rhythms so bright.

With every waltz, the branches sway,
Maples whisper, "Come dance, don't delay!"
In moonlit fun, all creatures play,
    Under the stars, they laugh and sway.

Gnarled Narratives

Once a gnarled oak, wise and old,
Shared tales of sea and riches untold.
Its branches creaked, but not from weight,
From the laughter of squirrels who often debate.

"Who's the fastest? Come take a spin!"
Squealed one little chipmunk with a twinkle and grin.
The oak shook its limbs; a wise old man,
"Speed isn't everything—have a fun plan!"

Beneath its knots, secrets unfold,
Of roots that tangled and stories bold.
A beaver brought logs, said, "Let's build a dam!"
The oak chuckled, "Make it cute as a clam!"

When storms rolled in, the oak would sway,
And say, "Hold tight, we'll dance the day away!"
Its gnarled narratives, mixed with delight,
Always kept spirits lifted and bright.

Symphony of Shadows

In the twilight, shadows play,
With trees that dance in a humorous sway.
Branches stretch and twist with glee,
Creating shapes of whimsy, just for me.

A playful fox leaps from the dark,
With a wagging tail, oh what a lark!
While shadows giggle, the owls hoot,
A symphony begins, oh how it's cute!

The winds join in with a gentle hum,
Flowing through leaves, oh, what's to come?
A concert of rustles, sweet serenades,
Where bright-eyed critters frolic in parades.

As the night deepens, they all gather near,
With creatures of humor, spreading the cheer.
In this shadowy world, laughter resounds,
In nature's concert, happiness abounds.

Dance of the Fallen Leaves

Leaves twirl down from the trees,
Like dancers shaking their knees.
They whisper jokes as they swirl,
With a giggle, they give the world a twirl.

Crispy crunch beneath your feet,
As squirrels plan a nutty meet.
They plot to steal the acorn crown,
While the wind laughs, spinning around.

A leaf tries to ride on a kite,
But flutters away in a comical flight.
The breeze giggles, 'what a sight!'
As it twirls into the night.

In the forest, antics unfold,
With tales that never grow old.
The trees chuckle, keeping a score,
As nature dances forevermore.

Nature's Diary

Look at the critters with their paws,
They're writing tales with nature's claws.
A raccoon scribbles by the stream,
Composing stories like a dream.

A squirrel's angst over lost nuts,
Makes diary entries full of guts.
While birds complain of noisy haters,
With tweets that sound like elevators.

The sun peeks in with a bright grin,
While clouds shout, 'Let the fun begin!'
Nature giggles, it's quite the show,
With every critter stealing the flow.

At dusk, the pages fill with laughs,
As all share tales of silly gaffes.
Each little creature with a quirk,
Makes the wilderness the best place to work.

Breath of the Wilderness

In the woods, the air's a mess,
Filled with giggles and leaf-dressed dress.
Mice are playing hide and seek,
While owls chuckle at their cheek.

The trees breathe out a funny tune,
As branches sway, making room.
Nature can't help but snicker,
As the sun makes shadows flicker.

A deer trips over a root, oh dear!
But laughs it off, with a quick cheer.
The breeze whispers, 'that was grand!'
As flowers giggle, hand in hand.

With every breath, a tale to tell,
In the wilderness, all do well.
Where laughter floats on the air so bright,
Making every moment feel just right.

The Conifer's Lullaby

In the pine trees, a soft hum flows,
Whispering secrets that everyone knows.
A squirrel's lullaby starts to play,
As the sun begins to sway.

The bears snore, in cozy nests,
While owls hoot, counting their zests.
They laugh as the wind comes to tease,
Swaying branches with the greatest ease.

A rogue pinecone drops with a thud,
Smiling as it rolls in the mud.
The squirrels cheer, 'what a show!'
While the wise old tree starts to glow.

Nature's symphony, full of grace,
With every sound, there's a smile on a face.
The conifers sing through the night,
In lullabies of pure delight.

Beneath the Canopy

Squirrels in bowties, they dance with glee,
Chasing shadows, just wait and see.
A ladder to nowhere, up to the sky,
As gumdrops fall from a passing pie.

Here comes a raccoon, in search of a snack,
In a top hat, with a keen little knack.
He plays the banjo, oh what a sight,
As the trees sway and join him tonight.

The Cedar's Secret

In the heart of the woods, a secret unfolds,
Where cedar trees whisper, their stories untold.
There's a rabbit named Fred, with a penchant for jokes,
He cracks them for owls and giggles with folks.

A squirrel named Linda swears she once saw,
A toucan in slippers, breaking the law.
With a wink and a nod, she shares her delight,
As they all gather round by the shimmering light.

Enchanted Echoes

Echoes of laughter bounce off the trees,
As birds wear cool shades, feeling the breeze.
A hedgehog on skateboards, zooming around,
Rolls past a porcupine, he stumbles, then bound.

At twilight, they gather, a quirky parade,
With pinecone cocktails, plans beautifully laid.
They sing silly songs, their voices entwined,
In the forest of mirth, where fun's never blind.

Stories Written in Sap

Beneath the big pines, a young turtle writes,
Of moonlit encounters and whimsical sights.
With sap for ink, he scribbles away,
Of bees playing poker, what a fine day!

A bear in a tutu starts to dance,
With a tutu-clad deer, they take a chance.
As the stories unfold, wild and absurd,
The laughter of critters is always heard.

Leaves of Lament

Leaves fell down with quite a clatter,
Squirrels laughed, saying, "What's the matter?"
A gust blew by, stole hats away,
They boiled my soup! These leaves can play!

Dancing trees with arms so wide,
In the wind, they twist with pride.
"Catch my hat!" the shouted calls,
But laughter echoes; none recalls!

Nature's jokes are never bland,
A branch that tickles, oh so grand!
The forest hums a silly tune,
With leaves that flop like cartoon balloons!

So here's to woods that play and tease,
Where laughter sways with every breeze.
Let's celebrate this leafy jest,
In the chaos, we find our best!

Roots That Bind

Roots deep down, they twist and tangle,
Whisper jokes in their leafy jangle.
They grip the earth with a silly face,
Bickering who's the strongest base!

"I'm the backbone!" one roots claim,
"No, I'm the top dog!" they stake their fame.
But up above, the branches roll,
Shouting, "Guys, you're not in control!"

Then came a raccoon, bold and spry,
He danced on roots as if to fly.
"Hey everyone, let's shake a leg!"
With groans, the roots began to beg!

Laughter ripples through the ground,
In tangled webs, joy can be found.
So wiggly roots, with each embrace,
Tell tales of fun in the wild space!

Boughs of Memories

Boughs stretch high as stories soar,
Each ring a tale, forevermore.
But wait, what's that? A bird goes "boop!"
Memory clouds with a silly swoop!

A crow that caws with a chuckle loud,
Brags of missing acorns in the crowd.
"I ate them all!" he fluffs his chest,
While squirrels plot to put him to jest!

Raccoons peek with clever eyes,
Joining in on the feathered lies.
Chasing echoes through the leaves,
Each branch holds laughter that never leaves!

So raise a glass to boughs that swing,
Sharing giggles the forest brings.
In every whisper and playful gale,
Are memories wrapped in a funny tale!

Above the Underbrush

Above the underbrush, shadows sway,
While critters plot their sneaky play.
A chubby hedgehog with a puffed-up back,
Said, "Move along, no room for slack!"

A rabbit bounced, quite full of cheer,
"Who's the king of this tall grass year?"
With paws on hips, he struck a pose,
While butterflies giggled, posing doze!

The wise old owl, a watcher keen,
Witnessed all in this funny scene.
"You silly folks, you crack me up!"
He hooted loudly, with quite a sup!

Nature giggles as fun times brew,
In bushes thick, and skies so blue.
From undergrowth to soaring heights,
Laughter echoes through the nights!

Glistening Dewdrops

In the early morn, they shine bright,
Dewdrops giggle, a sheer delight.
They tickle the leaves, dance on the grass,
Whispering secrets as breezes pass.

A critter hops by, slips with a splash,
Landing right in, with a comical crash.
The dewdrops chuckle, what a sight to see,
As the rabbit hops out, all wet and free.

A ladybug blinks, unsure of her fate,
Slides on a leaf, oh it's too late!
The laughter erupts from the glistening crew,
In this morning wonder, where joy is the brew.

Glistening orbs, on the edge of a leaf,
Leave behind trails of giggles, not grief.
In this playful world where trouble is few,
Every dawn brings joy, oh what a view!

Twilight Under the Treetops

As the sun dips low, laughter starts to bloom,
Creatures emerge from the evening gloom.
A raccoon with snacks, his grin ever wide,
Says, "Would you care for a popcorn ride?"

Squirrels are scheming, planning a race,
With acorns as fuel, they're quick to embrace.
A wise old owl hoots, gives them a chance,
"Watch me spin, boys, let's start a dance!"

Comparing their hops, they tumble and fall,
Rolling down hills, oh, they're having a ball.
The moon chuckles softly, lighting their play,
In twilight's warm grip, they chase fears away.

With giggles and squeaks, the night feels alive,
Underneath the stars, the spirit will thrive.
So let's raise a toast, with berries in hand,
To the twilight fun, where dreams take a stand!

Roots of Memory

Beneath the old oak, tales start to sprout,
The roots hold the laughter, what's life all about?
With every soft breeze, stories unfold,
Of gnomes playing tricks, oh so bold.

A squirrel recalls, with a cheeky grin,
The time he hid nuts, only to begin
A treasure hunt, with birds on his team,
But they feasted away, not knowing the scheme!

The mushrooms chuckle, in the patch so neat,
Swapping their secrets, who's got the best treat?
As shadows lengthen, the laughter retains,
The roots of good times grow in the plains.

With giggles still echoing through the old bark,
Memories linger, they'll leave quite a mark.
Nature it seems, loves a good jest,
In the roots of our hearts, laughter feels best.

A Journey Through Green

Oh, what a trip through the forest so bright,
With frogs telling jokes, and butterflies in flight.
We stumble across a snail, moving too slow,
He smiles and insists he'll just take it slow.

Down by the creek, the fish splash a tune,
Bubbles form laughter under the moon.
A chipmunk joins in, with a clap of his paws,
Declaring a party, woodlands applause!

The trees sway gently, sharing their laughs,
While branches tickle shy, little calf's.
Every step is a dance, every path filled with cheer,
In this green, gleeful world, nothing to fear!

As the sun sets low, our journey winds down,
We'll carry these giggles, wear joy like a crown.
Through valleys and hills, let's come back again,
For in laughter and friendship, the fun never ends!

Chronicles of the Grove

In the grove where squirrels chatter,
A raccoon steals a picnic platter.
The trees stand tall, they gently sway,
Their branches laugh at the fray.

A wise old owl with glasses thick,
Spouts wisdom mixed with a silly trick.
He hoots and hollers, 'Don't be a fool!
Dance like a leaf, that's the golden rule!'

The deer wear ties, oh what a sight,
They waltz at dusk, until the night.
The bushes gossip and giggle so,
While fireflies join in the glow.

When twilight falls, the fun doesn't cease,
The raccoons parade, embracing peace.
In the grove where laughter blooms,
Nature's humor surely looms.

Song of the Spruce

Oh, the spruce wears a cap made of snow,
And dances around with a twirl and a throw.
The pine cones laugh, rolling down the hill,
Their merry antics bring smiles, such a thrill!

The squirrels play tag, oh what a chase,
With acorns flying all over the place.
A chipmunk proclaims, 'I'm the fastest of all!'
But trips on a nut and takes a great fall.

"Let's arm wrestle!" the fir challenges loud,
But the spruce just chuckles, "You'll make me so proud!"

With arms wide open, the forest joins in,
A humorous ruckus, where fun will begin!

The sun starts to set, and stars twinkle bright,
The trees sing a tune to end the night.
In harmony, they sway and unite,
For the song of the spruce echoes in delight.

The Silent Watchers

In the stillness, the trees stand so wise,
Watching the antics beneath their skies.
The rabbits hop around in a race,
While whispers of wind tickle their face.

The owls wink knowingly at the hare,
'You'll trip on a root! Oh, be aware!'
The squirrels debate who can swing the best,
As the branches creak, they put it to test.

Beneath the canopy, shadows they play,
While leaves wear crowns like it's grand ballet.
The ruckus of critters, a joyous feat,
And the trees giggle in their silent seat.

The moon rises high, casting light on the fun,
The woodland party has only begun!
The silent watchers share laughter so sweet,
As nature's own crew taps their feet.

Carved by Time

Once a young sapling, the old tree shone bright,
Now with wisdom, it stands day and night.
Its bark tells tales of storms and of glee,
Of table manners used by a buzzing bee!

A raccoon once claimed it as a throne,
Adorned with moss and a pine cone alone.
He held court there, telling tales of grand,
While ants served drinks, all part of the plan.

The carved rough edges mark the years passed,
With laughter and tears that were gathered and cast.
The foxes gossip of love in the breeze,
While the owl chimes in with wise little pleas.

Oh, how time sings as the forest grows old,
With stories etched deeply, forever retold.
In the heart of the wood where the funny resides,
Each ring in the trunk hosts a light-hearted ride.

Beneath the Boughs

Squirrels plot their nutty heists,
Arguing who's the best at feasts.
Rabbits hopping, chasing flies,
While owls roll their ancient eyes.

A deer in shades, a fashion show,
In forest green, they steal the show.
Frogs croak jokes all night long,
As crickets strum their merry song.

Forest Guardians

A raccoon wears a little mask,
In the night, it's quite the task.
Badgers digging, what a mess,
But that's the way they like to dress.

Porcupines with quills so proud,
Secretly draw a little crowd.
They laugh and jest under the moon,
Claiming it's an afternoon!

The Language of Leaves

Leaves whisper secrets in the breeze,
Telling tales, bringing tease.
A pine tree giggles, sways with glee,
Mocking the maples, 'Look at me!'

The wind joins in, a playful tease,
Tickles the branches, shakes the trees.
With every rustle, every sigh,
It's nature's way to laugh and fly.

Secrets of the Sylvan Realm

In the glade, a dance takes flight,
Mice in shoes, oh what a sight!
Bears with banjos strum a tune,
To the rhythm of the bright full moon.

Foxes gossip, dreams to share,
While hedgehogs lounge without a care.
A forest joke goes round and round,
And laughter echoes, all around.

Whispers in the Canopy

Squirrels wear hats, think they are kings,
Chasing their tails, laughing at springs.
A raccoon in boots, what a sight to behold,
Stealing my lunch, so brave and so bold.

The owls keep gossip, perched high on a limb,
Who knew they could chatter, their voices so grim?
While branches all sway, in a dance with the breeze,
The trees shake their heads, as they laugh with such ease.

A chipmunk recites poetry beneath a tall pine,
His audience, crickets, all hold their wine.
They sip from acorns, with giggles and cheers,
Celebrating life, for several long years.

At twilight they gather, the forest has grown,
For a karaoke night, oh how they have shone!
The laughter, so loud, wakes the deer from their dreams,
In the heart of the woods, wacky joy ever beams.

Echoes of the Ancient Woods

In shadows of giants, a jester appears,
Juggling with mushrooms, to the crowd he cheers.
A bear with a bowtie, strutting with glee,
Claims he's the finest, 'I'm a sight to see!'

The trees stand like judges, with wise old faces,
While bushes are giggling in hidden places.
A fox on a tricycle makes quite a scene,
Zipping around, all part of the routine.

The wind tells a joke, to the leaves in their dance,
While hedgehogs in tuxedos waltz in a prance.
Laughter in echoes, through the pines it does roll,
Nature's own comedy, filling each soul.

With insects as chorus, they hum a sweet tune,
Under the glow of the mischievous moon.
Through laughter and fun, the night softly weaves,
Tales of the woods, where humor believes.

Song of the Silent Pines

The pines have a secret, they giggle in green,
With whispers of tales, never quite seen.
A porcupine's party, with balloons in the air,
Dancing with fireflies, without a care!

A grumpy old turtle plays cards with the bees,
While frogs in the pond sing, 'We aim to please!'
The fungi all clamor for a chance at a role,
In a soap opera, full of drama and soul.

The winds crack a joke, causing branches to sway,
The chipmunks all chuckle, as they scurry away.
A raccoon in shades, sipping juice from a jar,
Claims he's the star of this bizarre bazaar.

As moonlight drips laughter upon leafy heads,
The creatures all gather, ignoring their beds.
For under the pines, where silliness thrives,
The song of the night, keeps joy in our lives.

Beneath the Canopy's Embrace

A squirrel in slippers, what a fancy sight,
Rolling on acorns, oh what pure delight!
With jokes in their pockets, each critter, they play,
The forest's a circus, come join the fray!

The winds blow a tune that tickles the leaves,
While rabbits in coats share their fanciful weaves.
An owl with a monocle, wise and quite spry,
Reads stories of naps, to the clouds in the sky.

Odd little mushrooms, in a dance so divine,
Form circles of laughter, quite wobbly and fine.
The trees hum along, their bark seems to grin,
In the echoes of laughter, joy always begins.

As night softly falls; oh, the antics don't end,
A parade of silliness on which all depend.
Beneath the grand canopy, hilarity reigns,
In the heart of the woods, where fun ever reigns.

A Tapestry of Twigs

In the forest deep, a twinkle did sprout,
The squirrel wore boots, danced all about.
Frogs in top hats debated the news,
While a raccoon served snacks, with fancy shoes.

Woodpeckers tap, like playing a beat,
Dancing on branches, oh so sweet!
A rabbit sang high, a fox joined in,
Their chorus so loud, it made the trees grin.

The owl hooted softly, a critic so wise,
"Less sass in your tails, or I close my eyes!"
But who could resist, in this merry old place,
Where giggles and wiggles filled every space.

So gather your friends, the mischief is ripe,
A tapestry woven with laughter and hype.
In the woods where the antics run wild and free,
Even a tree can laugh—just wait, you will see.

The Spirit of the Forest

In shadows they dance, the spirits so sly,
Tickling the branches as the winds pass by.
With shades made of laughter, they twirl and they leap,
While mischievous critters plot tricks and a peep.

A raccoon, all dressed in his fanciest threads,
Juggled acorns while perched on his head.
The pixies played pranks, with giggles abound,
As the curious deer looked, puzzled, around.

The riverkeeps splashed in a silly parade,
Chasing their tails, they found joy unafraid.
Amidst the tall trees where the whispers arise,
The spirit of fun wears no visible guise.

So if you wander where the laughter is heard,
Know fun is the language, not just in a word.
The spirit of joy, like leaves doth unfurl,
In the forest of giggles, come give it a whirl.

Beneath the Branches

Beneath the branches, where shadows do play,
The squirrels tell secrets in their own silly way.
With acorns as hats, they plot out their schemes,
Dreaming of forests filled with soft, syrupy dreams.

A hedgehog with glasses reads under the boughs,
While a snail in a bowtie gives all of his vows.
"Eat more greens!" he proclaims with a cheer,
As chipmunks all cheer with a loud, raucous jeer.

In the depths of the woods, a party ensues,
With fungi for cake and the best dance shoes.
The owls are the judges, their wisdom is sage,
But their laughter makes everyone stay on the stage.

So swing on the vines and glide on the breeze,
Join in the frolics, do whatever you please.
Beneath the branches, the joy's out of sight,
In this laughter-filled vale, the woods are just right.

Pinecone Prophecies

The pinecones all gathered, a mystical bunch,
Discussing the future over a sweet lunch.
"Will winter be long? Will spring take a chance?"
With giggles they shared a prophetic dance.

A wise old owl hooted, "Oh, have you not heard?
The winds will blow swift, like a jubilant bird!
The bunnies say summer will bring a nice treat,
With berries and sunshine—let's all grab a seat!"

The roots laughed and whispered, in gossiping glee,
While the fawns joined the gossip, all wild and free.
"Will they start a parade?" asked a curious tree,
"Only if we promise to hang out with glee!"

So pinecones conspired with leaves in the air,
Crafting a future full of joy and good fare.
In a world sprinkled with laughter, dreams take flight,
Where pinecone prophecies bloom, oh, what a delight.

Under the Aged Arbors

Beneath the crooked branches, we roam,
A squirrel in sunglasses, claiming the dome.
Chasing after shadows, we trip and we fall,
The trees are all laughing, they're having a ball.

A woodpecker shouts, 'Hey, that's my snack!'
While we share a picnic, munching on quack.
The ants form a conga, they dance on the mat,
While the old oak just chuckles, 'Imagine that!'

Relics of the Redwood

Among the giants, we spot a shoe,
Is it lost or a relic? It's hard to construe.
A squirrel decides it's his brand-new hat,
Now he's strutting around, looking silly and fat.

With knots that tell stories and bark like old fees,
We find ancient knowledge in whispers of leaves.
The raccoons hold court, in their honorary place,
Trading tall tales with a smirk on their face.

The Dance of Dappled Light

Sunbeams are winking, playing peek-a-boo,
The mushrooms are grooving, as if they just knew.
A rabbit does ballet, pirouette and twirl,
While the shadows all giggle, giving it a whirl.

The grasshoppers chirp in a rhythm so bright,
Hosting a concert in the warm evening light.
While beetles do backflips off fungi that sway,
Nature's odd dance, where everyone plays.

Hidden Life Above

Look up, my friend, at the leaves on high,
A family of owls, just watch how they fly.
They hoot out jokes, and they pass silly notes,
While the finches all laugh, wearing colorful coats.

A raccoon in pajamas is scaling the trees,
Swapping old stories with a honeybird tease.
"Who would have thought there's such fun in the skies?"
A squirrel shouts back, "It's a life full of highs!"

The Lullaby of the Mountain Breeze

A tickle from the wind so sly,
Whispers of a bird flying high.
Squirrels chatter, gather their loot,
As trees dance in their leafy suit.

Laughter echoes through the tall pines,
Where even the rocks have silly signs.
The brook giggles, flows with glee,
Singing secrets only it can see.

Clouds wear costumes of fluffy white,
Playing hide and seek, what a sight!
The sun winks with radiant rays,
Joining in the forest's playful plays.

In this merry land where critters roam,
Every corner feels just like home.
So listen close, and you might hear,
Nature's lullaby, oh so dear.

Stories Stitched in Bark

Upon the trunk, the tales are found,
Whispers scratched in bark abound.
A bear once tried to ride a bike,
Now he just walks, a funny hike.

The chipmunk writes with acorn ink,
Of the time the owl tried to think.
It got so lost in its own mind,
It hooted out a joke unkind.

A raccoon stole a chef's old hat,
Confused it for a welcome mat.
Now he cooks up meals bizarre,
Fried grasshoppers in a jar.

From every ring, a laughter shared,
In this forest, none are spared!
So gather 'round, come take a look,
At the tales etched in every nook.

The Journey of the Wandering Elm

An elm decided to go roam,
Leaving behind its cozy home.
It packed a bag with leaves and dreams,
Off to explore, or so it seems.

It met a pine wearing glasses tight,
Debating if it was day or night.
The elm just chuckled, 'Join my spree!'
They danced through woods so wild and free.

Together they bumbled through the glade,
Hiccups of laughter, plans unmade.
A fox joined in, with a tail so proud,
Making poetry that sounded loud.

At night they toasted with fireflies,
Under starry swirls and sighs.
With every step, a new giggle spun,
Their journey gleefully just begun.

Reveries of the Gnarled Oak

There's a gnarled oak, wise and old,
With branches that shake like stories told.
It dreams of squirrels in hats so grand,
That host tea parties in the sand.

Once, it fancied becoming a boat,
Sailing fish with a playful float.
Breeze tickled bark, oh what a scene,
The great oak laughed, once so keen.

Frogs croaked jokes like bouncing balls,
While crickets chimed with laughter calls.
The oak just nodded, swayed with pride,
Such funny visions never hide.

To rattle leaves is its only quest,
In this world where giggles rest.
With a wink, it sways to dreams anew,
A merry heart for all to pursue.

www.ingramcontent.com/pod-product-compliance
Lightning Source LLC
Chambersburg PA
CBHW071813160426
43209CB00003B/67